LILY & VAL

EST. 2012

Life OF THE *Party*

PAPERCRAFTING

DESIGN ORIGINALS
an Imprint of Fox Chapel Publishing
www.d-originals.com

Welcome
TO THE PARTY!

This book provides you with the ready-made papercrafting materials you need to throw a wonderfully coordinated event. All of the elements are beautiful as standalone pieces, but feel free to add some personal touches!

You can use your own words, embellish with other crafting materials, and combine cards with scrapbook paper designs to create beautiful pieces. Pick the designs that are just right for your party, and let your creativity flow!

Valerie McKeehan is the Founder & Creative Director of Lily & Val, a Pittsburgh-based boutique stationery and lifestyle brand, and author of the best-selling book *The Complete Book of Chalk Lettering*. The Lily & Val brand continues to be an expression of Valerie's penchant for nostalgia and sentimentality, capturing the simple beauty of ordinary life. Memories of days well-spent or days long since past inform and inspire much of her work. Through her whimsical and iconic designs, she encourages others to live creatively, passionately, and in tune with the simple pleasures of life from the ordinary to the extraordinary. Her work has been featured throughout the national press including *Martha Stewart Living, Good Housekeeping, Food Network,* and *Good Morning America* with corporate clients such as Starbucks, Macy's, and *Flow Magazine.*

PROJECT IDEAS

CRAFTING MATERIALS

CARDS

You can use the cards in this book as invitations, greetings, thank-you cards, or anything else. Try mounting the art on top of a scrapbook paper card to give it a new border. Or decorate an art card with gorgeous pens, glitter, or embellishments. Experiment with different combinations!

Writing an invitation? In addition to important details such as where and when the party will be, include any information your guests will need. For example, think about the physical address, parking instructions, who is hosting the event, a phone number and deadline for RSVPs, a time for the party to end, and anything your guests might need to bring (a bathing suit? a potluck dish?).

ENVELOPES

Need an envelope for one of the cards in this book? They're simple to create. Before you start, copy or trace one of these envelope templates. Laminate it or paste it to thick poster board to ensure that it will last a long time.

HOW TO ASSEMBLE AN ENVELOPE

Trace your envelope template onto your favorite piece of double-sided scrapbook paper. Cut it out.

Referring to the dashed lines on the template, create the shape of the envelope by first folding the two side flaps in toward the center, then folding in the bottom flap. Use a bone folder, if you have one, for neater folds.

Tape the bottom three folded flaps of the envelope together, leaving the top flap free to open and close. If you plan to hand deliver your envelope to its recipient, you may place the tape on the inside, where it will be hidden. If you want to mail your envelope, reinforce it with extra tape on the outside seams of the flaps to ensure that it doesn't come open in transit.

You're all done—add a stamp and send the card!

Small TEMPLATE

The large envelope is a standard size and should be happily accepted and mailed at your local post office.

Large
TEMPLATE

BELLY BANDS

These versatile decorations add a sophisticated touch to your table. Use them to label food, menus, or anything else. Or, as here, use them to suggest conversation starters!

  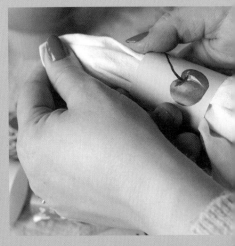

NAPKIN RINGS

Punch out the napkin rings beginning on page 35, and embellish them (optional). Bend a ring into a circle and tape together on the back side. Use it to hold your napkin in place. Roll your napkin or, for a simple gather:

- Fold the napkin in half diagonally.

- Pinch it at the center point of the fold and lift it up, letting the corners fall naturally.

- Slip on the napkin ring.

- Set the napkin on the plate or table and arrange the edges.

MENUS

The menus beginning on page 39 are ready to use and/or embellish. Put one by your buffet, dessert table, or appetizer tray to let your guests know what kind of cookies you've made and how you suggest they pair their cheeses. Put one by your bar area if you have a signature cocktail that requires mixing. Or use one to list what's for dinner! Note: This is a great opportunity to call out any dishes that contain allergens, if your guests need to know.

COASTERS

Turn to page 43 for perforated, ready-to-use coasters. To make more permanent square coasters, pick up some tiles from a DIY supply store; 4" x 4" works well. Cut squares to fit the tops using the scrapbook paper patterns starting on page 81. Spread a water-based sealer such as Mod Podge on a tile and affix the paper square to it. Smooth it out, making sure there are no folds or bubbles and the paper is aligned properly. Spread more sealer on the top of the scrapbook paper, making a smooth finish. After the coaster has dried, cut a piece of thin cork to the same size as the tile and glue it to the bottom.

WINE CHARMS

If your party involves mingling, wine charms will prevent your guests from mixing up their drinks. Punch out the wine charms starting on page 43 and leave them by the bottle with a pen. Or decorate them yourself ahead of time!

When writing on a dark background, try a white gel pen, paint pen, or metallic pen or marker.

MINI CARDS AND TAGS

The cards starting on page 51 and the tags starting on page 63 can be used as gift tags, favor tags, buffet tags, or any other small, pretty labels you need. Punch them out and, for the tags, carefully cut off the corners with a sharp pair of scissors. Use a hole punch to add a hole if you want to use ribbon or twine to tie the tag to something. Just like cards, these tags are lovely enough to stand alone, but they can become mini masterpieces with just a few added elements. You can use the same ribbons, gemstones, charms, and layered effects you used to make cards.

PLACECARDS

Placecards are a classy, beautiful way of assigning seating. Simply punch out the cards starting on page 69, letter them, fold them into tents, and arrange around your table as table numbers or individual name tags.

In addition to naming the dishes you're serving, buffet tags are a great place to note their ingredients for your guests who need to know. Think of who'll be attending, and add "vegetarian," "contains nuts," "gluten free," or other qualifiers that might answer their questions.

ANNIE

MENU

MIMOSA BAR
FRUIT CUPS
QUICHE
SPINACH SALAD

Let's
Brunch

Bon Appétit!

On the following pages you'll find everything you need to make gorgeous crafts—hand-lettered, illustrated, perforated, colored, and all ready for you! Just go for it and don't stress about whether you're doing it "right." Pour your heart into your work, have fun with it, and the result will be beautiful! Enjoy!

Sweet as Candy

treat yourself

Sugar & SPICE

hello Sweetie

hello
Sweetie

Sugar
&
SPICE

treat
yourself

Sweet
as
Candy

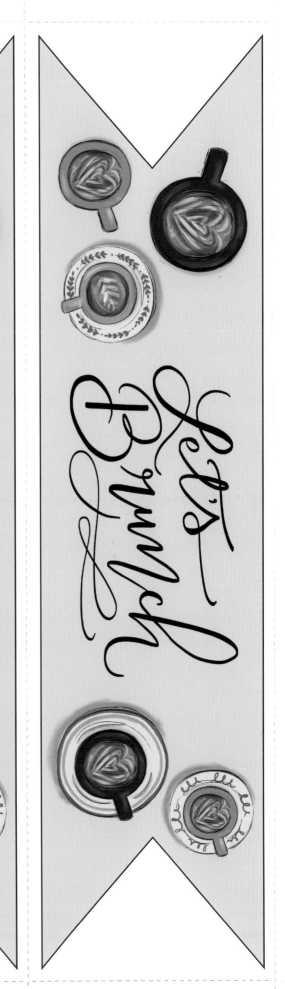

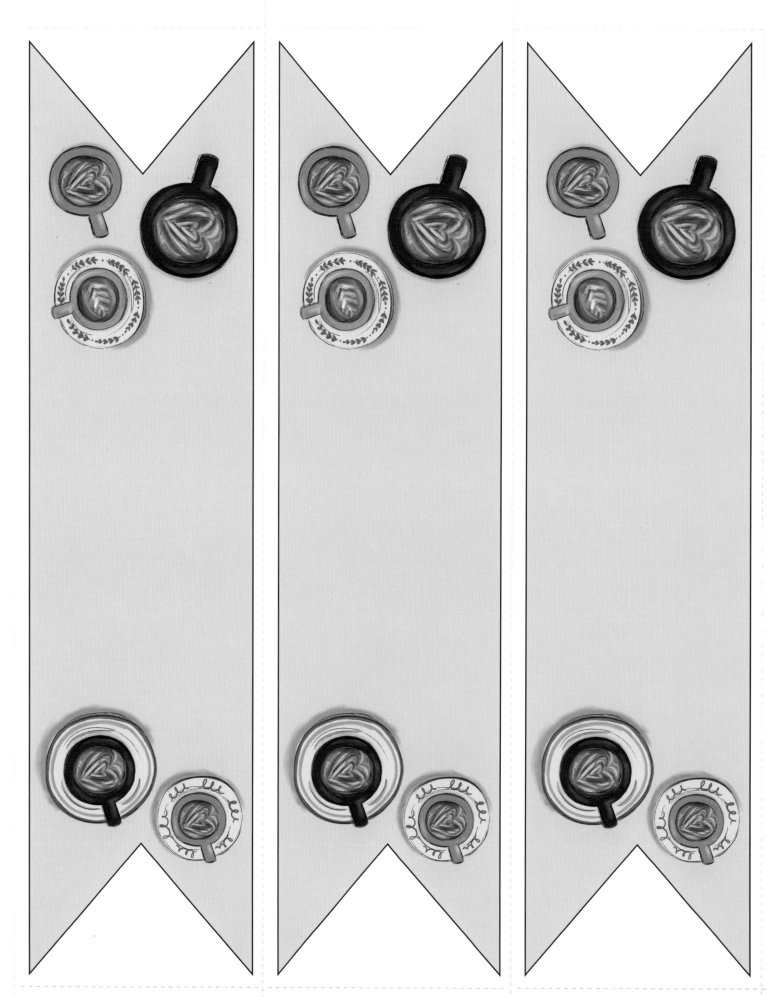

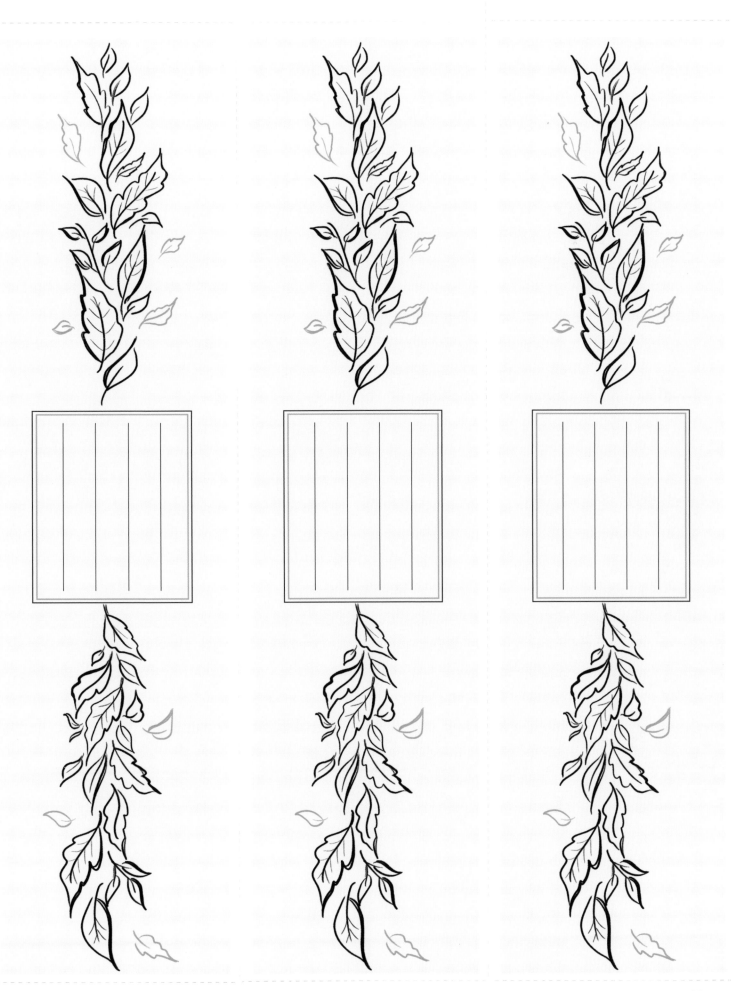

Menu

Menu

Menu

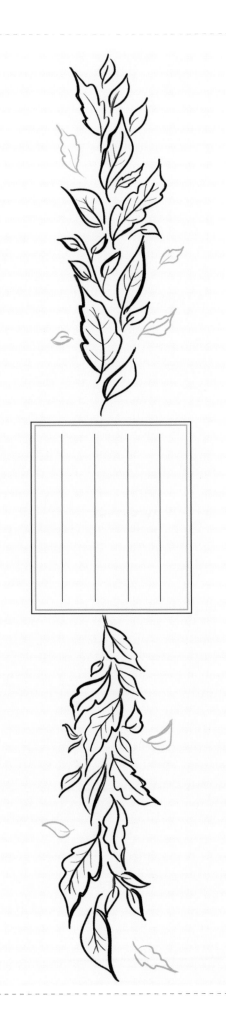

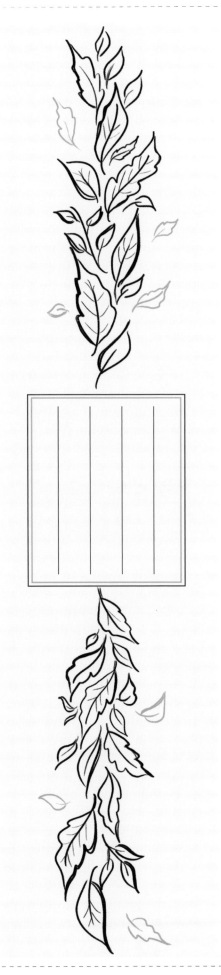

Menu

Menu

Menu

MENU

MENU

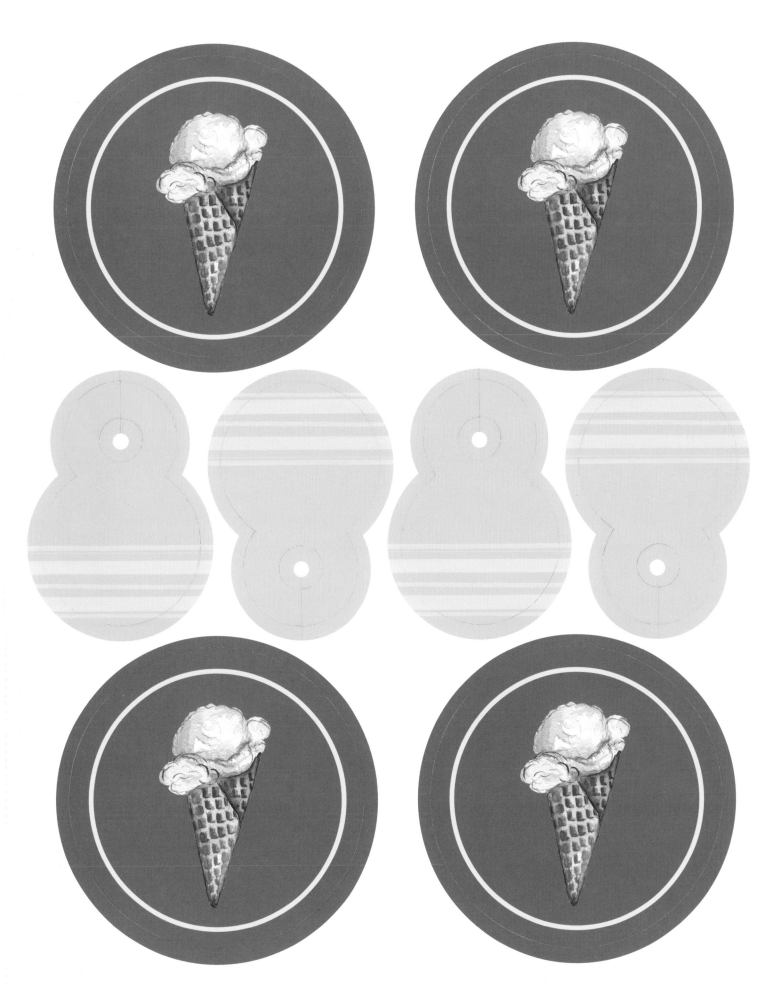

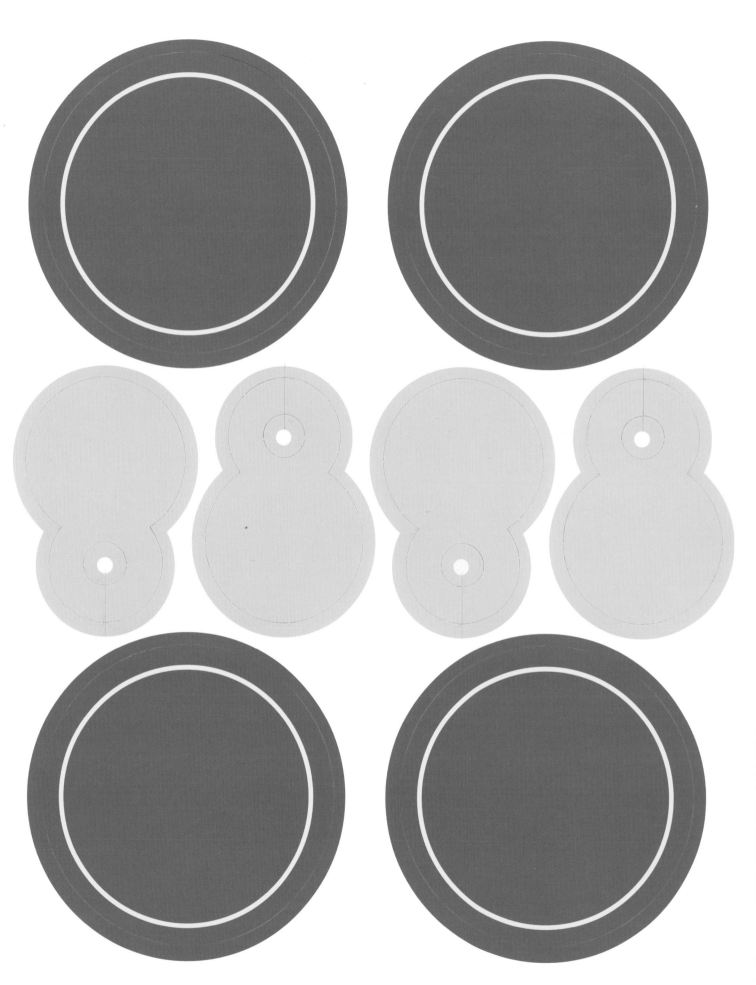

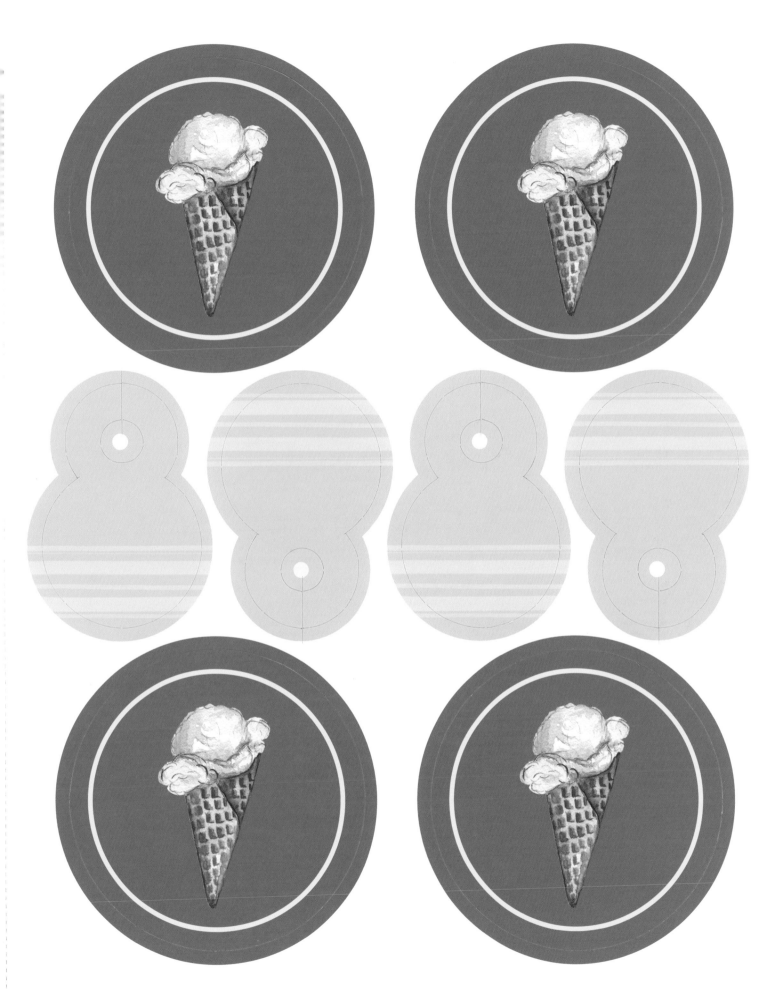

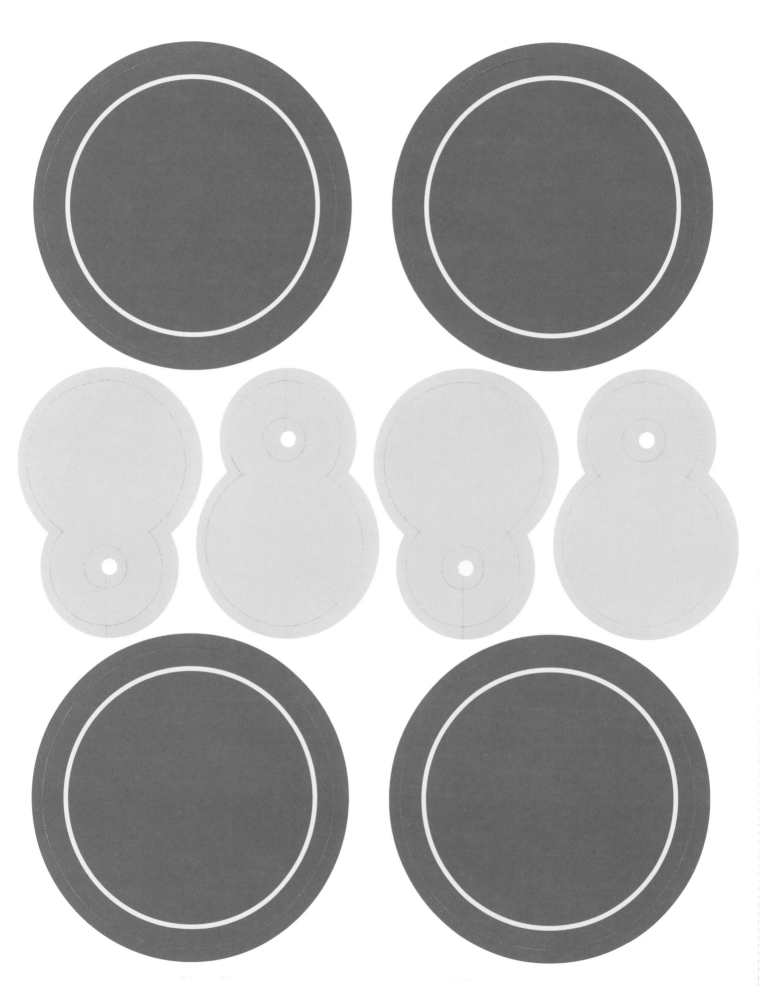

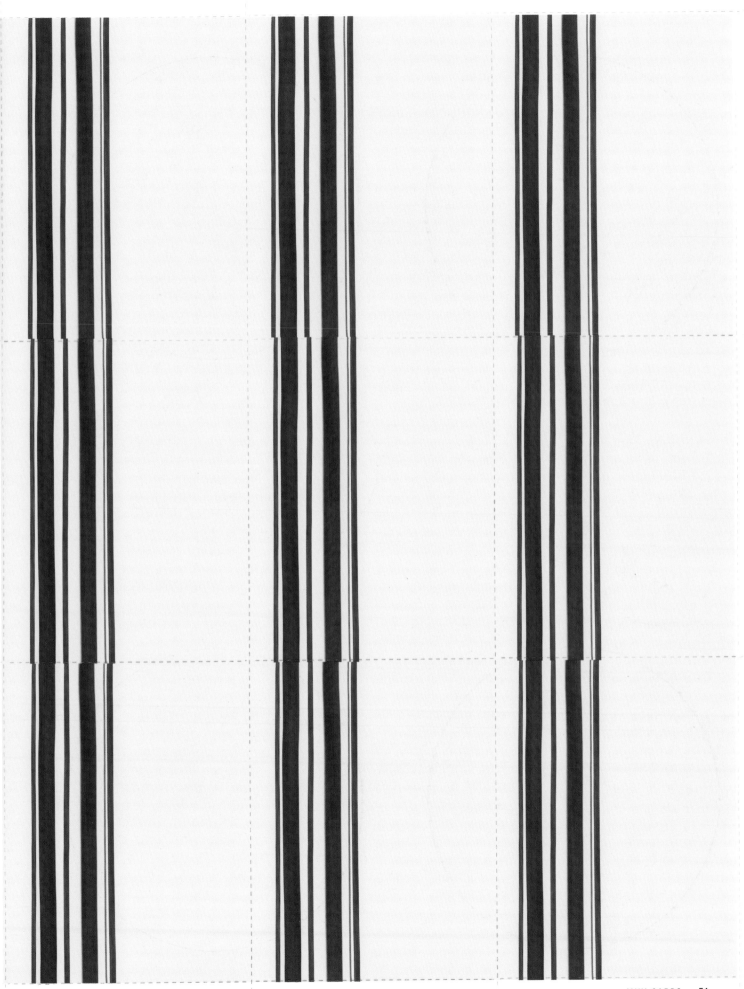

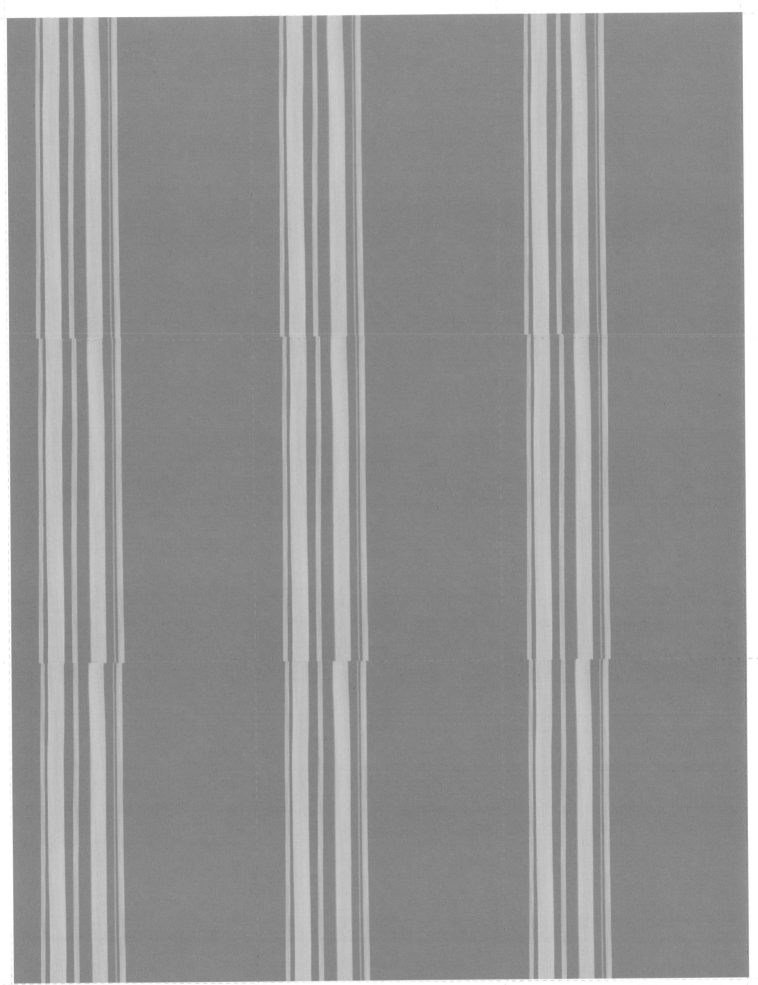

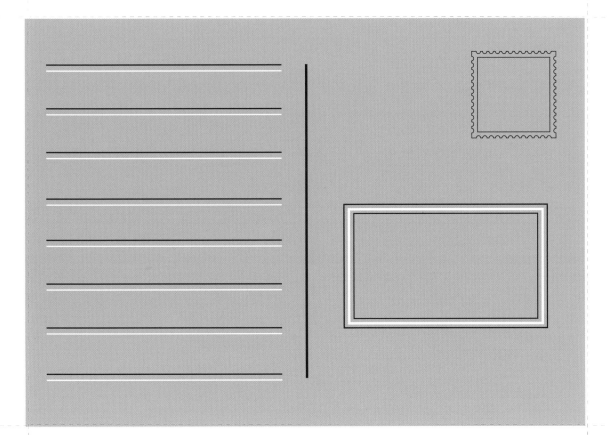

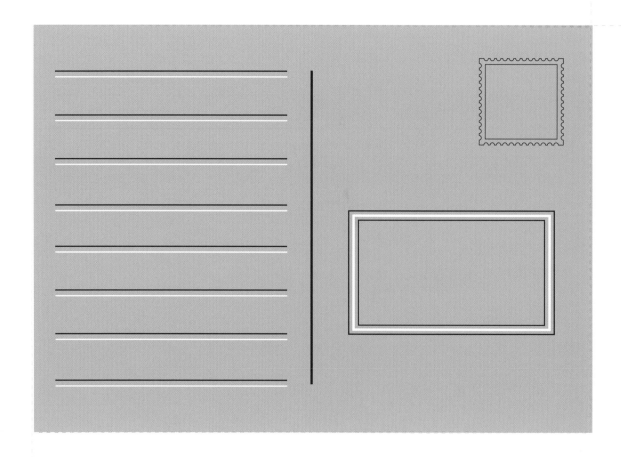

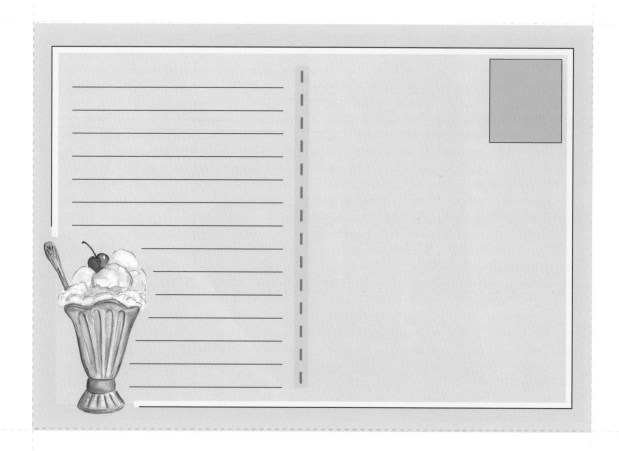

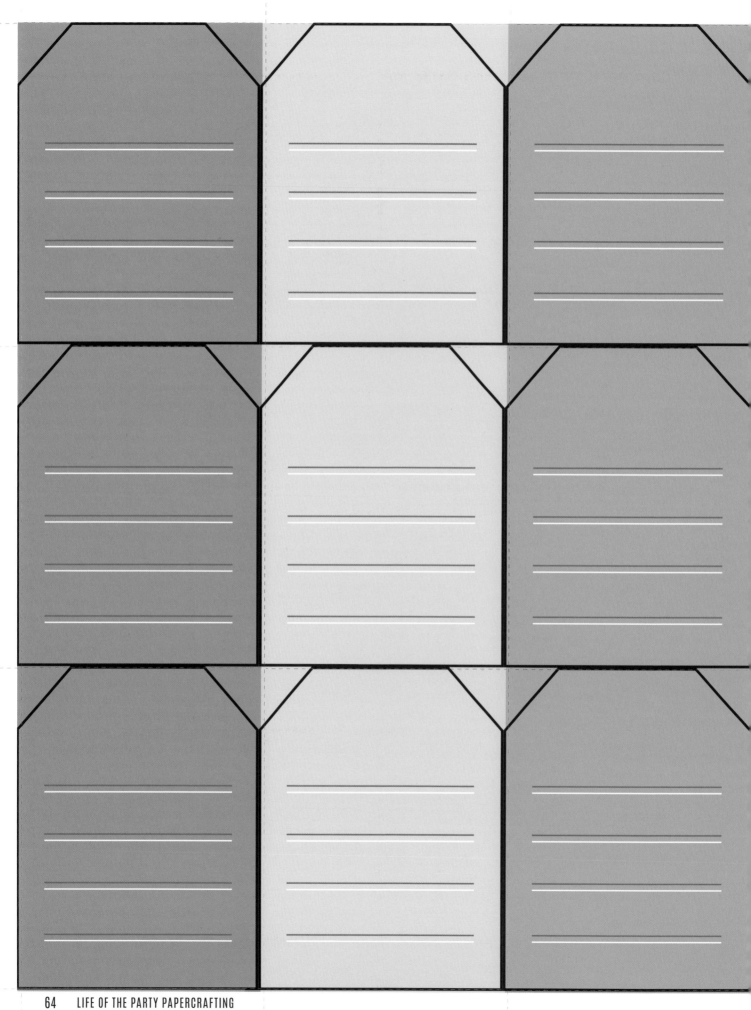

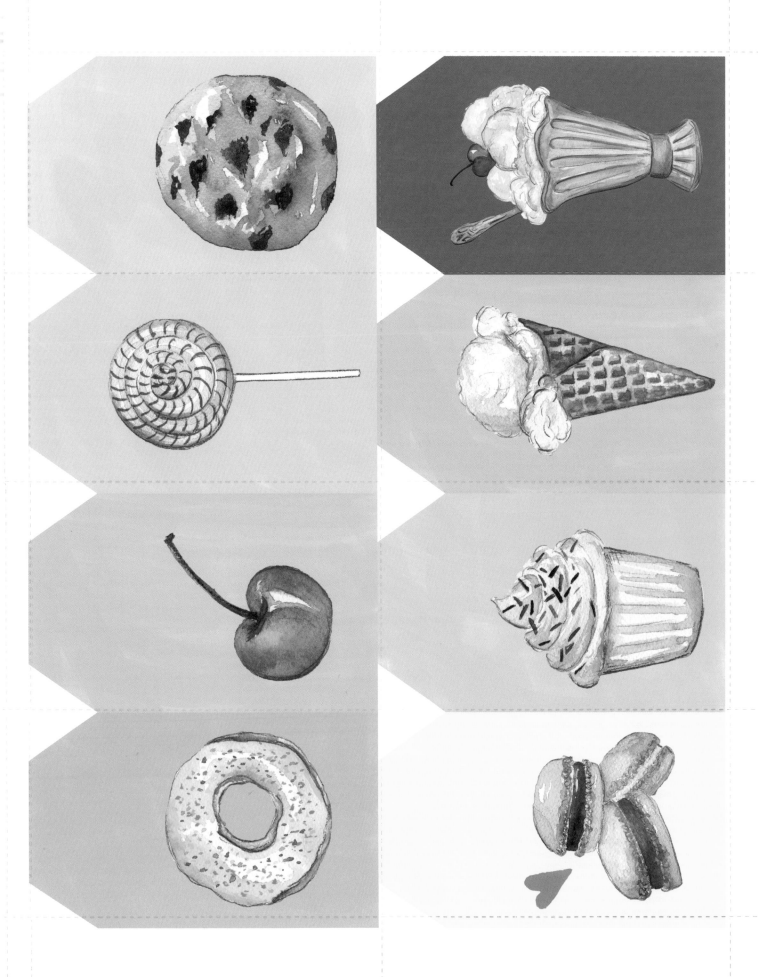

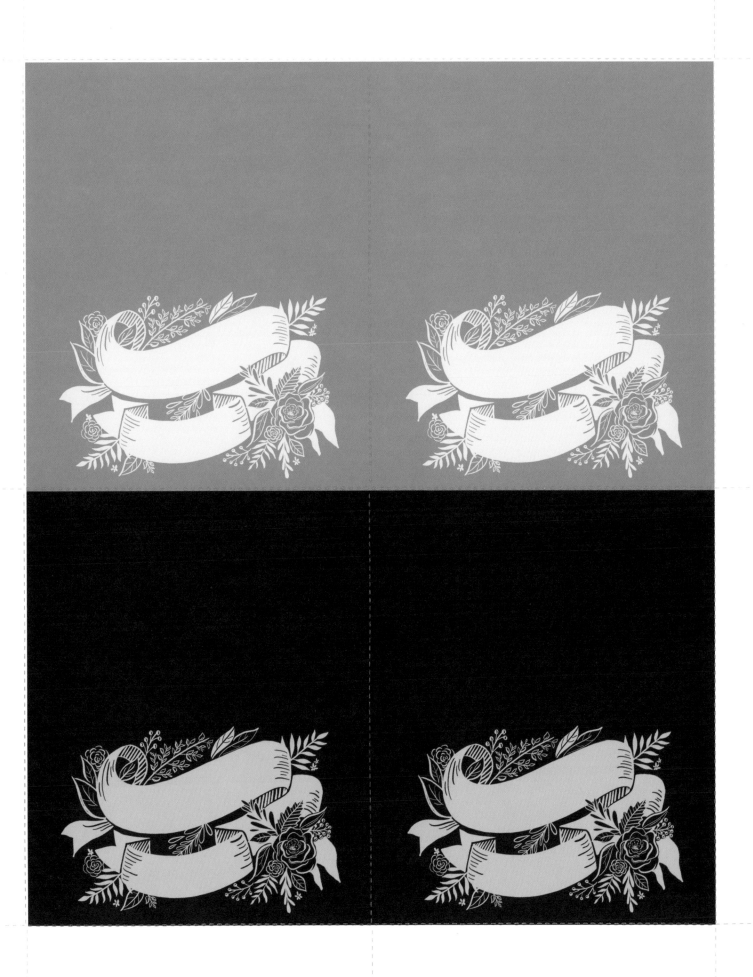

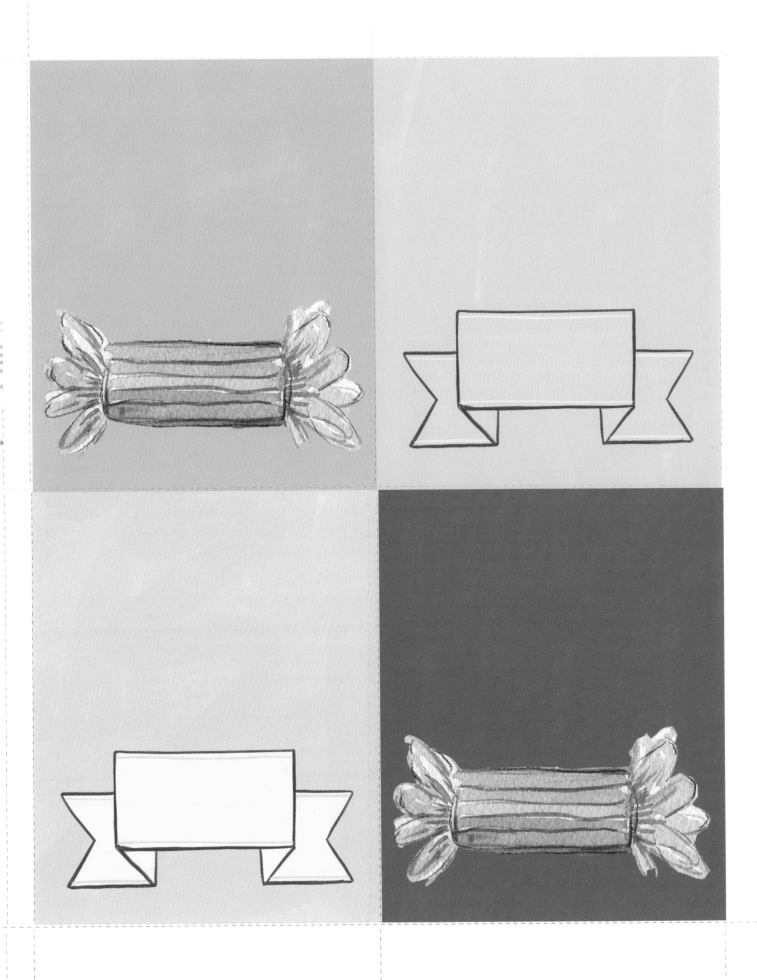

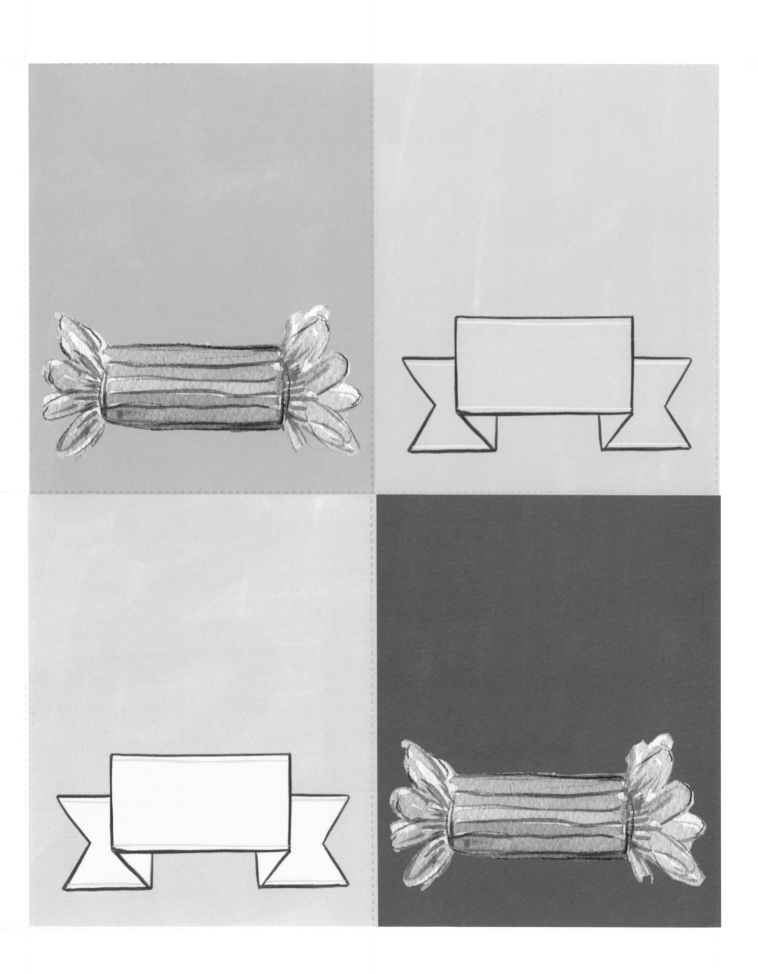

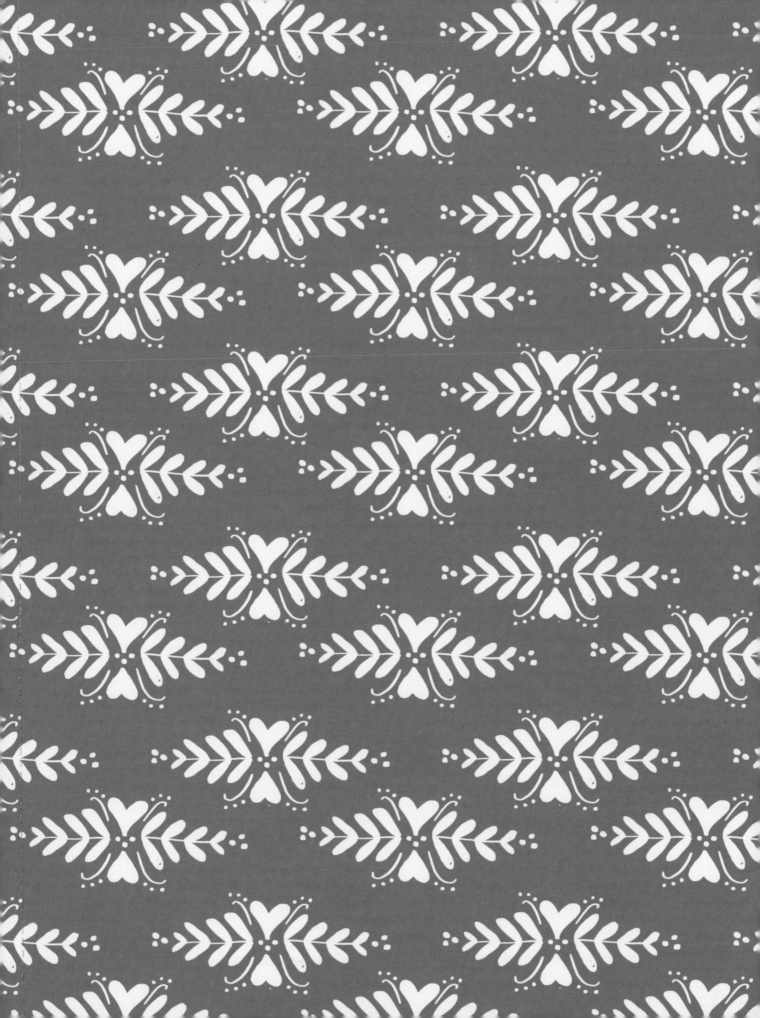

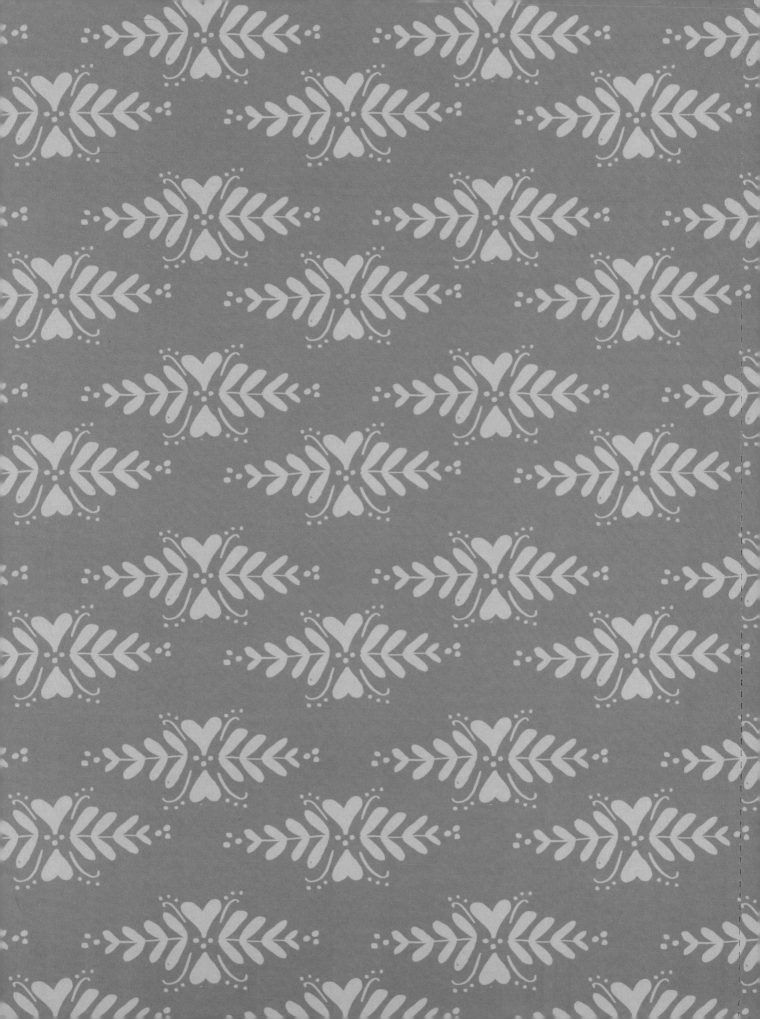